PHYSICAL MAPS

ALL OVER THE MAP

Ellen Rodger

Crabtree Publishing Company
www.crabtreebooks.com

Crabtree Publishing Company

www.crabtreebooks.com

Author: Ellen Rodger
Publishing plan research and development:
  Sean Charlebois, Reagan Miller
  Crabtree Publishing Company
Series editor: Valerie J. Weber
Editors: Valerie J. Weber, Kelly McNiven, Reagan Miller
Proofreaders: Barbara Kiely Miller, Crystal Sikkens, Jessica Shapiro
Editorial director: Kathy Middleton
Project manager: Summit Kumar (Q2A Bill Smith)
Art direction: Joita Das (Q2A Bill Smith)
Design: Roshan (Q2A Bill Smith)
Cover design: Ken Wright
Photo research: Ranjana Batra (Q2A Bill Smith)
Production coordinator and prepress technician: Katherine Berti
Print coordinators: Katherine Berti, Margaret Amy Salter

Photographs:

Cover: Wikimedia Commons: NASA (tl), NOAA (cl), Wikimedia Commons: NOAA (bl), Anton Balazh/Shutterstock (br); P1: Shutterstock; P4: Lithiumphoto/Shutterstock; P5: Malgorzata Kistryn/Depositphoto (b); P5: Patrick Poendl/Shutterstock (tr); P6: Michael Schmeling/Alamy; P7: Nationalatlas.gov (t); P7: Trappe/Caro/Alamy (b); P8: Education Images/UIG/Getty Images; P9: Hadrian/Shutterstock; P10: Rich Lasalle/Age Fotostock/Getty Images; P11: Nikonaft/Shutterstock; P12: jgorzynik/Shutterstock; P13: Prometheus72/Shutterstock; P15: Wessel du Plooy/Shutterstock; P16: Digital Data Services; P17: Arid Ocean/Shutterstock; P18: Richard I'Anson/Lonely Planet Images/Getty Images(tr); P18: mypokcik/Shutterstock (bl); P19: jiawangkun/Shutterstock; P20: NASA; P21: Sam DCruz/Shutterstock(t); P21: jakobradlgruber/Shutterstock (b); P22: Dorling Kindersley/Getty Images; P23: Arsgera/Shutterstock(tr); P23: Planet Observer/Universal Images Group/Getty Images(bl); P24: DEA/R. MERLO/De Agostini Picture Library/Getty Images; P25: Kvadrat/Shutterstock(t); P25: CandyBox Images/Shutterstock(b); P26: The Natural History Museum/Alamy; P27: Getty Images News/Getty Images (tr); P27: Dr. Ken Macdonald/Science Photo Library (b); P28: Gary Hincks/Science Photo Library; P29: NOAA/NGDC/Science Photo Library (c); P30: Wikimedia Commons (map); P30: iofoto/Shutterstock (girl); P31: istockphoto/Thinkstock (l); P31: Wikimedia Commons (r)
Q2A Art Bank: P14–15

t=top, tr=top right, tl=top left, cl= center left, bl= bottom left, br=bottom right, b=bottom, l=left, r=right

Library and Archives Canada Cataloguing in Publication

Rodger, Ellen
    Physical maps / Ellen Rodger.

(All over the map)
Includes index.
Issued also in electronic format.
ISBN 978-0-7787-4492-4 (bound).--ISBN 978-0-7787-4497-9 (pbk.)

    1. Maps--Juvenile literature. 2. Map reading--Juvenile literature.
I. Title. II. Series: All over the map (St. Catharines, Ont.)

GA105.6.R64 2013   j912   C2012-908256-2

Library of Congress Cataloging-in-Publication Data

Rodger, Ellen.
  Physical maps / Ellen Rodger.
      pages cm. -- (All over the map)
  Includes index.
  ISBN 978-0-7787-4492-4 (reinforced library binding) -- ISBN 978-0-7787-4497-9 (pbk.) -- ISBN 978-1-4271-9330-8 (electronic pdf) -- ISBN 978-1-4271-9318-6 (electronic (html))
  1. Maps--Juvenile literature. I. Title.
  GA105.6.R625 2013
  912--dc23

                                    2012048518

Crabtree Publishing Company

Printed in the USA/052013/JA20130412

Published in Canada
Crabtree Publishing
616 Welland Ave.
St. Catharines, ON
L2M 5V6

Published in the United States
Crabtree Publishing
PMB 59051
350 Fifth Avenue, 59th Floor
New York, New York 10118

Published in the United Kingdom
Crabtree Publishing
Maritime House
Basin Road North, Hove
BN41 1WR

Published in Australia
Crabtree Publishing
3 Charles Street
Coburg North
VIC, 3058

CONTENTS

Why Are Maps Useful?

Maps are detailed drawings of Earth. There are many different kinds of maps. Some maps show an area's states, cities, or roads. These maps can help us find where we are going. Some maps give us information about the world we live in. For example, a map can show what kind of foods are grown in a certain country or **continent**.

▲ *This hiker is using a map to find his way through the forest.*

Physical maps show the natural features of an area such as mountains, oceans, and lakes. A physical map might also show **glaciers**, deserts, plains or **plateaus**.

Glaciers are slow-moving rivers of ice. Some physical maps show their location and give information on their size.

Maps have been used for many years to find the location and details of an area. This map of the world was created hundreds of years ago.

ANCIENT MAP

Physical Maps

Physical maps show the physical features found on Earth. Physical features are **landforms** created by nature. Some landforms are small, such as hills. Other landforms are large, such as mountains and plains.

Some physical maps also include features built by humans. These features can include buildings, roads, and bridges.

--------- LANDFORMS OF THE UNITED STATES ---------

Cascades

Rocky Mountains

Great Plains

Superior Great Lakes

Huron Ontario

Michigan

Erie

Sierra Nevada

Central Lowlands

Appalachian Mountains

Atlantic Ocean

Coastal Plain

Pacific Ocean

Gulf of Mexico

▲ This map of the United States shows large landforms such as the Rocky Mountains and Great Lakes.

We need physical maps to define areas of land. A physical map of the Rocky Mountains shows us where the mountains are located. It also shows us the cities and towns around them.

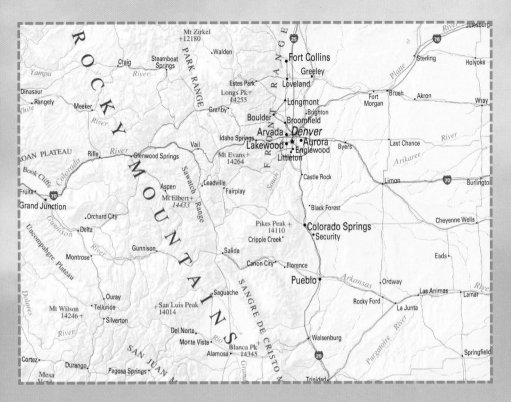

The Rocky Mountains run more than 3,000 miles (4,828 km) through the United States and Canada.

These soldiers are using a physical map to learn about the landforms near their military base.

Making Physical Maps

Making physical maps requires skill and a lot of information about our planet. Some information comes from **surveys** of the land.

Other information comes from photographs taken from cameras attached to the bottom of airplanes. The airplane flies along a planned path. The camera takes many images of the same area. Each image shows a slightly different view. These pictures are called **aerial photographs**.

Mapmakers use many images of an area to create a physical map.

Mapmakers use a tool called a **stereoscope** to look at aerial photographs. A stereoscope acts like 3-D glasses. Mapmakers view two photographs of the same area taken at different angles. The photographs partly lie on top of each other. The stereoscope gives a **three-dimensional** view of the landscape. This view shows the landforms and features that go on a map.

With a stereoscope, this photograph would appear three-dimensional. Without one, the image looks blurry.

Mapmakers also use detailed photos of Earth taken from **satellites** in space to create physical maps. Satellites use many tools to gather information. Their computers can show exact locations of landforms on Earth. All of this information, called **data**, is used to make maps.

Maps used to be drawn by hand. Today, most maps are made on a computer. Computer maps are called digital maps.

GIS is another tool used for making physical maps. GIS stands for Geographic Information System. It is a computer system for storing geographic and map information.

▼ *Maps made by computers have more details than maps drawn by hand.*

Thousands of satellites fly over Earth.
Many take photos to measure landforms.

Using Physical Maps

Physical maps show us what the land in an area looks like. **Engineers** use physical maps to plan where to build human-made structures such as roads and bridges. Look at the picture of the bridge below. Why would looking at a physical map be helpful for the engineer building this bridge? What kind of physical features would make it difficult to build a bridge?

▲ *Engineers studied physical maps before building this bridge across the river.*

Mountain climbers study a map on their climb.

Mountain climbers and hikers also use physical maps to plan their trips. A physical map shows climbers the **elevation,** or height, of the mountain they are climbing and what kind of **terrain** is found in the area. It can also show areas that can be dangerous or require special skills to climb such as a glacier. To safely climb a glacier, mountain climbers need to be prepared and know their location. A physical map provides climbers with this important information.

Physical Map Features

Physical maps pack a lot of information into a small space. To do this, mapmakers use **symbols** to stand for real mountains, rivers, and forests. Symbols can be simple shapes or drawings that stand for something. They can also be lines that represent a river or a road. Map symbols are explained in a box called a **legend**.

The legend on this map shows symbols that represent features, such as cities and mountains.

PHYSICAL MAP OF TENNESSEE

MISSOURI

Clarksville

Cumberland River

Nashville

Dyersburg

Kentucky Lake

TENNESSEE

ARKANSAS

Mississippi River

Jackson

Duck River

Murfreesboro

Columbia

Shelbyville

Memphis

Chattanooga

N

W   E

ALABAMA

MISSISSIPPI

Tennessee River

S

A map's **title** gives you information about what is being shown in the map.

Like most maps, a physical map also has a **compass rose**. The compass rose shows the four directions—north, east, south, and west. On the map below, find Nashville. What lake is found to the west of Nashville?

Hikers find their way by using a map and comparing it to the landforms around them.

KENTUCKY

Oak Ridge

Clinch River

Kingsport

Appalachian Mountains

Knoxville

NORTH CAROLINA

Great Smoky Mountains National Park

GEORGIA

Legend

★ state capital

● city

▲▲ mountains

☐ water

— state boundary

▬ national park

Map Facts

All the marks on a map are symbols, including lines that mark **borders**. Physical maps also use color as a symbol.

Scale on Physical Maps

The **scale** of a map shows how distance on a map relates to actual distance in the real world. For example, look at the physical map of the Denver, Colorado, area below. The scale explains that one inch (2.5 cm) on the map is equal to 40 miles (64 km) in actual distance. Approximately how far is Denver from the nearby city of Colorado Springs?

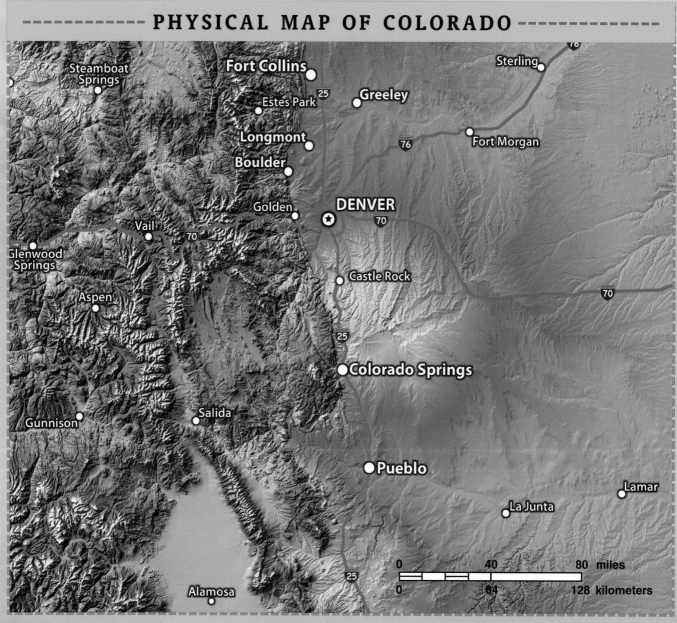

PHYSICAL MAP OF COLORADO

Steamboat Springs
Fort Collins
Sterling
Estes Park
25
Greeley
Longmont
76
Fort Morgan
Boulder
Golden
DENVER
70
Vail
70
Glenwood Springs
Castle Rock
70
Aspen
25
Colorado Springs
Salida
Gunnison
Pueblo
Lamar
La Junta
0   40   80 miles
0   64   128 kilometers
25
Alamosa

▲ *Find three cities that are within 40 miles (64 km) of Denver.*

Maps can be **large-scale** and **small-scale**. A large-scale map shows a small geographic area. The scale represents a smaller distance than on a map showing a larger area. For example, on a small-scale map, one inch might equal 100 miles (161 km). On a large-scale map, the same measurement might only equal one mile (1.6 km).

▼ *On this small-scale map, one inch represents more than ten times the distance than on the map of Colorado from page 16.*

PHYSICAL MAP OF THE UNITED STATES

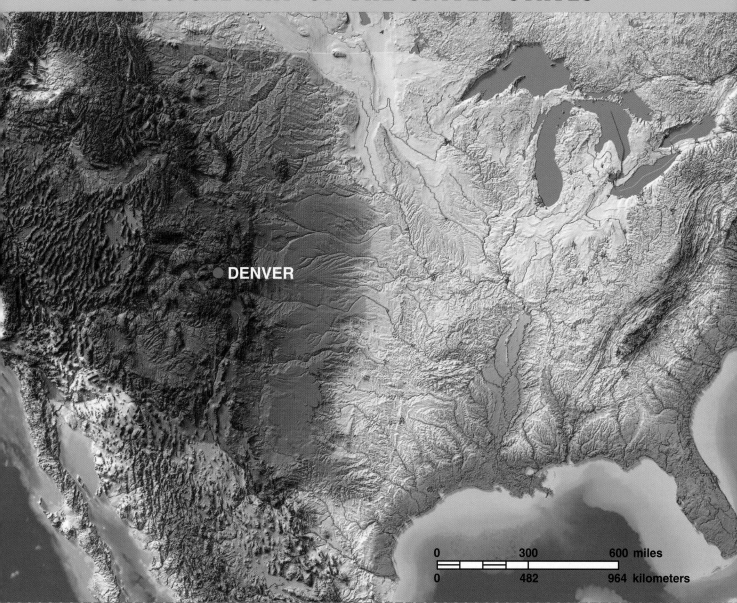

DENVER

0	300	600 miles
0	482	964 kilometers

Maps and Landscapes

Some physical maps show the **landscape** of a certain place. Landscapes are the visible features of an area of land. Landforms are one part of a landscape. Landscapes also include other features such as the buildings, trees, and roads. Some physical maps show the landscapes of large areas, such as an entire continent or country. Others show smaller areas, such as a national park or a forest.

Landscapes have a lot to do with how we live. How is the landscape of the area shown above different from the landscape of a busy city shown on the left?

Maps show an image of a landscape from above. Imagine you were looking down from a tall building. The street below you would seem small. You would see all of the street's landmarks scaled down in size.

This photo of the Lincoln Memorial in Washington, D.C., was taken from above. Everything looks smaller than it actually appears on the ground.

Landforms
on Maps

Earth's landforms vary in size and shape. Some physical maps use color and shading to show their shape and height.

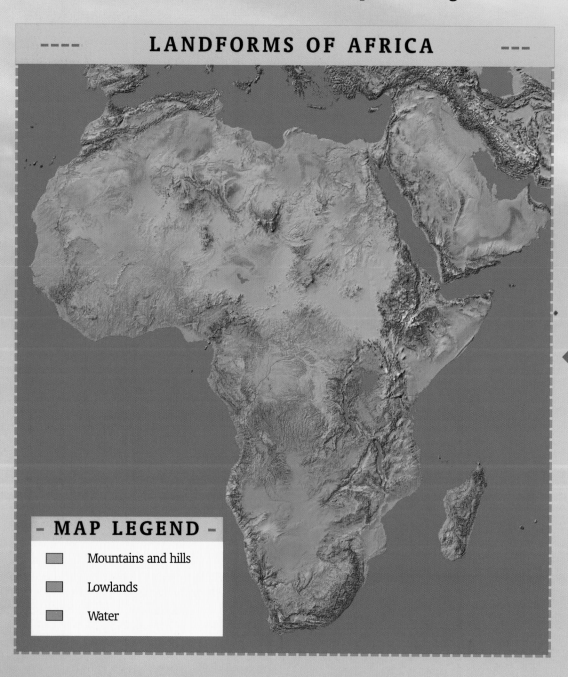

LANDFORMS OF AFRICA

- **MAP LEGEND** -
- Mountains and hills
- Lowlands
- Water

The legend on a landform map explains what each color represents.

There are many kinds of landforms. Mountains usually appear in groups called ranges. Plateaus are highlands between mountain ranges. Valleys, or lowlands, are low areas surrounded by hills or mountains. Broad, flat areas called plains lie along the coasts or inland on a continent.

Long, steep slopes are found in the Great Rift Valley in Kenya.

This picture shows the plains in southern Alberta located east of the Rocky Mountains.

Highlands
and
Lowlands

Physical maps show Earth's high points and low points. The height of a piece of land is called its elevation. High points include mountains and plateaus, or **flatlands**. Low points include marshes and valleys.

A detailed physical map shows low-lying coasts and tall hills in different colors.

----------- ELEVATIONS OF JAMAICA -----------

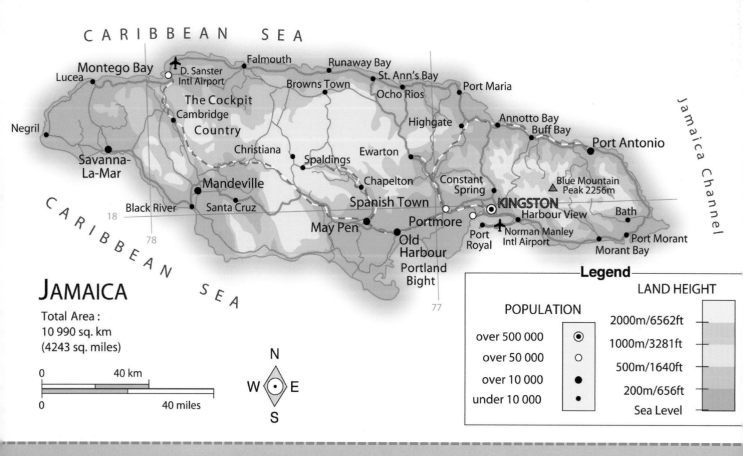

CARIBBEAN SEA

Lucea
Montego Bay
D. Sanster Intl Airport
Falmouth
Runaway Bay
St. Ann's Bay
Port Maria

The Cockpit
Cambridge
Country
Browns Town
Ocho Rios
Highgate
Annotto Bay
Buff Bay

Negril
Christiana
Ewarton
Port Antonio

Savanna-La-Mar
Spaldings
Blue Mountain
Peak 2256m

Mandeville
Chapelton
Constant
Spring
KINGSTON
Bath

Black River
Santa Cruz
Spanish Town
Harbour View

May Pen
Portmore
Port
Royal
Norman Manley
Intl Airport
Port Morant
Morant Bay

Old
Harbour

Portland
Bight

CARIBBEAN SEA

Jamaica Channel

JAMAICA

Total Area:
10 990 sq. km
(4243 sq. miles)

0 ——— 40 km
0 ——— 40 miles

N
W · E
S

Legend

POPULATION

over 500 000 ◉
over 50 000 ○
over 10 000 ●
under 10 000 ·

LAND HEIGHT

2000m/6562ft
1000m/3281ft
500m/1640ft
200m/656ft
Sea Level

A land's elevation is measured from sea level. **Sea level** is the height of the ocean where it meets land. Mapmakers measure a mountain's elevation from sea level to the top of the mountain. For example, Mount Everest in Asia is 29,029 feet (8,848 m) above sea level. The mountain's height was first determined during a **survey** made in 1856.

▲ *Mount Everest is the highest mountain on Earth.*

◀ *Satellite images show the elevation of Earth's landforms.*

Map Facts

Physical maps can show elevation with lines, shading, and color. Mountains look wrinkled. The coast may look flat and be shown in one color.

Topographic
Maps

A **topographic map** is a kind of physical map that shows elevation and slope in landscapes in three-dimensional (3-D) detail. Most topographic maps use contour lines to show changes in height. **Contour lines** are curved lines that join points of equal elevation. Lines that appear close together show steep areas while lines spaced apart show less steep slopes.

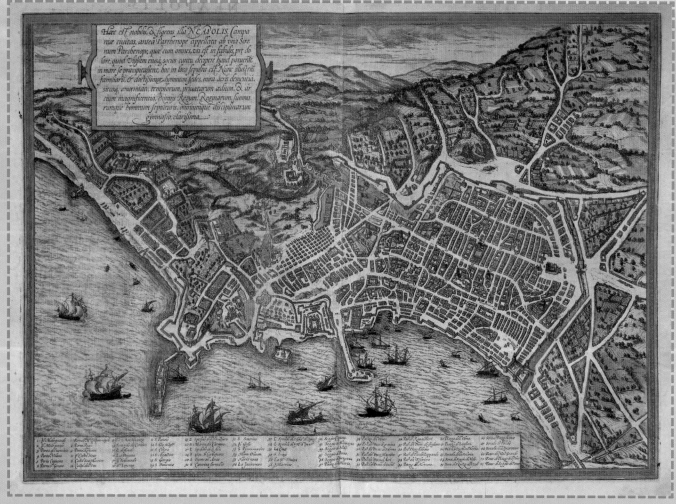

▲ Even in the 1500s, people made topographic maps.
Find the roads and hills on this map of Cologne, Germany.

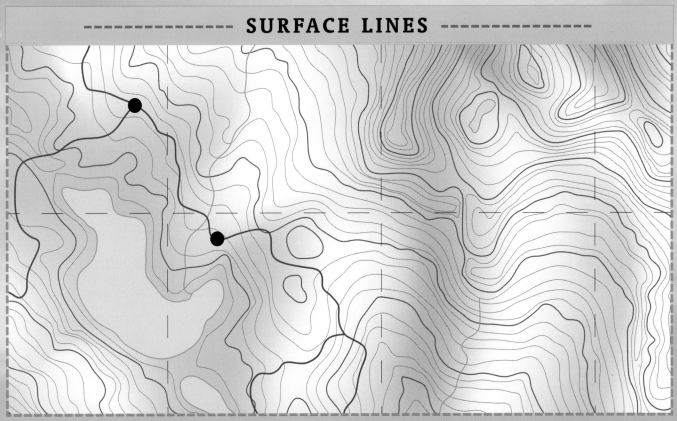

Topographic maps are made from measurements taken by surveyors. **Surveyors** measure the position of things.

▲ *Some topographic maps with contour lines look like puzzles. If you know the meaning of the lines, it is easy to understand the map.*

◄ *Surveyors use a number of tools to measure the landscape.*

Bathymetric
Maps

Bathymetric maps are a special kind of topographic map. Instead of showing landforms on land, they show natural features found on the bottom of a lake, bay, or ocean. Similar to topographic maps, bathymetric maps use contour lines to show elevation and depth.

▲ *This picture shows landforms at the bottom of the ocean. Do any of these landforms look similar to landforms you see on land?*

Mapping underwater landscapes is challenging for scientists because they cannot see what is below the water. Scientists use special equipment with **sonar** to find underwater mountains, volcanoes, canyons, and ridges.

An underwater volcano creates a new island landform. ►

◄ *This is a sonar image of the ocean floor. The colors in the legend show different depths.*

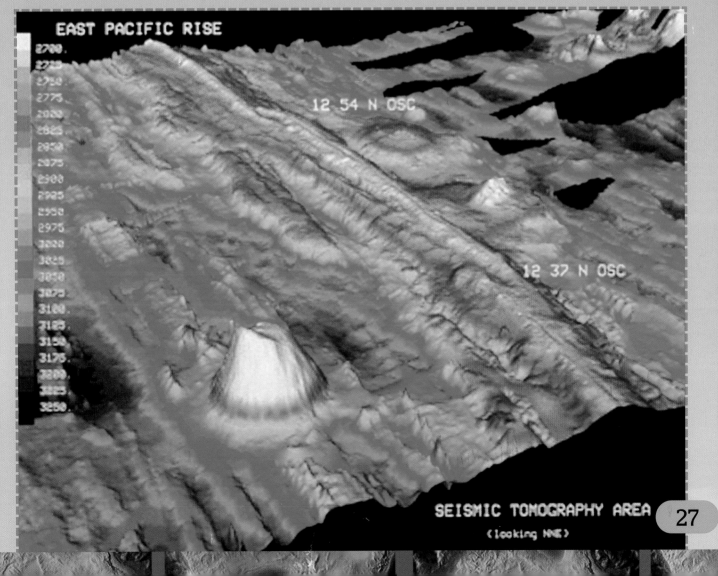

EAST PACIFIC RISE

2700.
2725.
2750.
2775.
2020.
2025.
2050.
2075.
2900.
2925.
2950.
2975.
3020.
3025.
3050.
3075.
3100.
3125.
3150.
3175.
3200.
3225.
3250.

12 54 N OSC

12 37 N OSC

SEISMIC TOMOGRAPHY AREA
(looking NNE)

Geologic Maps

All landforms begin with rocks. **Geologic maps** are a type of map that focus on the rock formations found beneath soil and plants. Some geologic maps also include natural features in their legend such as glaciers. Different colors in the legend show how old the rocks are in certain areas. The map below shows the geologic rock in Iceland created by volcanoes.

▼ *Which age of rock shows the most active volcanes?*

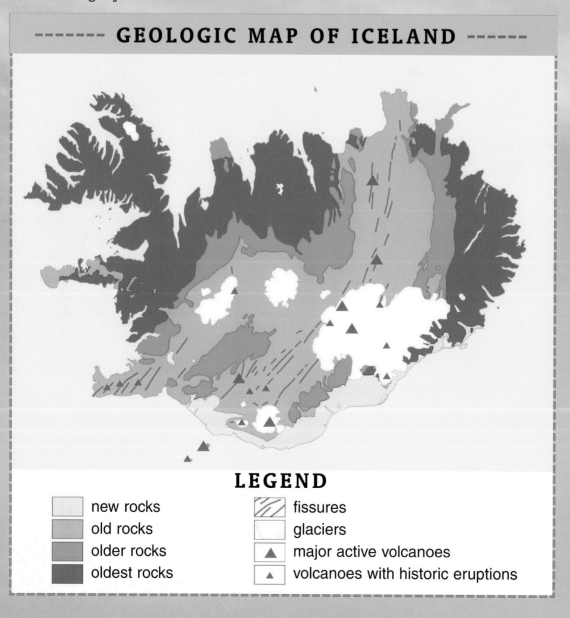

GEOLOGIC MAP OF ICELAND

LEGEND

- new rocks
- old rocks
- older rocks
- oldest rocks
- fissures
- glaciers
- ▲ major active volcanoes
- ▲ volcanoes with historic eruptions

Geologic maps are used for developing land and finding natural resources such as oil and water. They also show us areas that are more likely to experience earthquakes or landslides.

LANDFORM MAPS

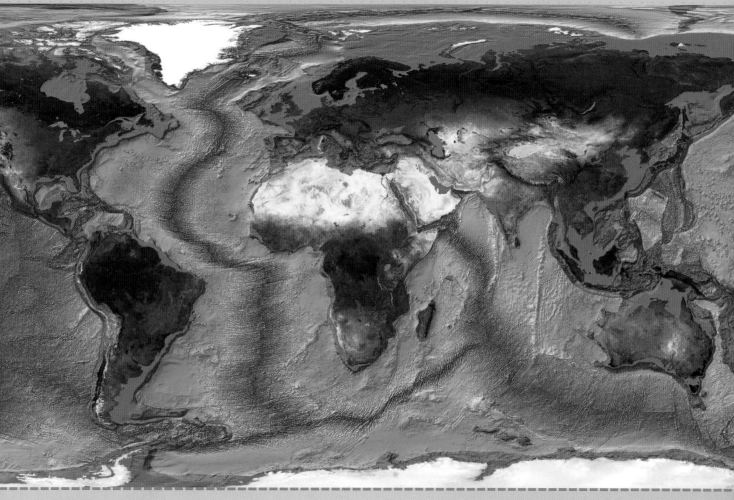

▲ The legend on this map shows the age of rock formations around the world.

MAP LEGEND

■ newly formed rock		■ 100 million years ago	
■ 40 million years ago		■ 220 million years ago	
■ 60 million years ago		■ 280 million years ago	

Mapping from Memory

Make a physical map of your country from memory. Ask an adult to help you find a good map of your country as a sample. You can copy the basic outline of the map from one you find in an atlas.

▼ *Study a map before you try to make it from memory. Try to remember where landforms are located. It is harder than you think!*

Study the map and make notes on the major landforms. Note where the bodies of water are, such as oceans and lakes. Where are the mountains and deserts? Draw the major landforms on your outline map. When you are finished, compare your map to the one you studied. Have you missed any major landforms?

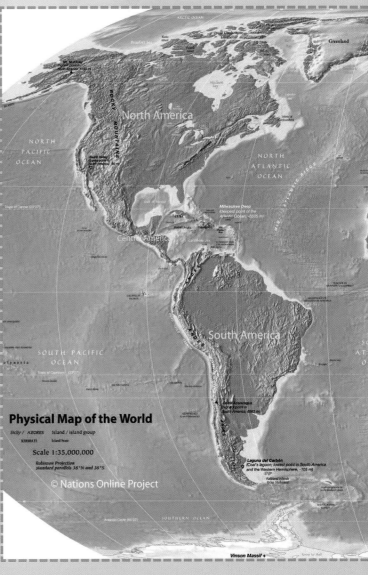

▲ Compare your map to the one you studied earlier. Do they look similar?

Glossary

Note: Some boldfaced words are defined where they appear in the book.

bathymetric map A map that shows the natural features of the bottom of a body of water, such as an ocean or river

border An outer edge or boundary

continent One of seven large landmasses on Earth

glaciers Slow-moving rivers of hard, packed ice located near mountains and at Earth's poles

landforms Physical features formed by nature, such as mountains or plains

landscapes The visible features of land, such as its hills, trees, and water sources

plateaus Areas of high ground that are level or flat

satellites Machines that orbit around Earth and collect information about the planet and space

sonar An instrument that uses radio waves to locate landforms or objects underwater

survey A record of an area or feature of land for map information

terrain The physical features of an area of land

three-dimensional Describes something that is not flat. Three-dimensional images can be viewed for length, width, and depth

Index